# Sweet Dreams, Wild Animals!

## A STORY OF SLEEP

EILEEN R. MEYER

ILLUSTRATED BY

LAURIE CAPLE

*Sweet Dreaming!*
*Eileen Meyer*

2015

Mountain Press Publishing Company

Missoula, Montana

For my siblings: Kathy, Terry, Sandra, and Jennifer. And for my old friends who are like family: Carol, Terri, Andy, Sue B., Sue W., Julie, and Sandy. Thank you for your support. —E.R.M.

For Ethan, Stephen, and Adelae. ♥ —L.C.

The illustrator would like to thank the staff members at the University of Minnesota Raptor Center, Minnesota Zoo, and Como Park Zoo and Conservatory. A special thanks to Colleen and Miss Lily, and Emily and Trin!

The author would also like to thank Scott Shaffer, San José State University.

Library of Congress Cataloging-in-Publication Data

Meyer, Eileen R., 1960- author.
 Sweet dreams, wild animals! : a story of sleep / Eileen R. Meyer ; illustrated by Laurie Caple.
   pages cm
ISBN 978-0-87842-637-9 (cloth : alk. paper)
1.  Sleep behavior in animals—Juvenile literature. 2.  Sleep behavior in animals—Juvenile poetry.  I. Caple, Laurie A. illustrator. II. Title.
 QL755.3.M49 2015
 591.5'19—dc23

    2014037551

Printed in Hong Kong by Mantec Production Company

MP Mountain Press
PUBLISHING COMPANY
P.O. Box 2399 • Missoula, MT 59806 • 406-728-1900
800-234-5308 • info@mtnpress.com
www.mountain-press.com

The sun has set; the sky is dark.
Bright stars shine in the night.
It's time to rest, to dream sweet dreams,
then wake with morning's light.

The animals will slumber, too.
Some near, some far away.
How will they settle down to sleep?
Each has a special way.

A wooly friend rests on a branch.
She eats and sleeps up high.
The soft wind whispers through the leaves
and sings her lullaby.

**Sweet dreams, koala.**

## Koala

This little tree dweller is active at night, munching on leaves after dusk. To sleep during the day, the koala finds a comfortable spot in the fork of a tree. It rests in a hunched position to stay warm in cold weather. Although the koala resembles a teddy bear, it is not a bear at all. Koalas, which are found in eastern Australia, belong to the same family as the kangaroo: the marsupials. Koalas eat plants and have dense wooly fur.

You close your eyes and drift to sleep—
that's something fish can't do.
Their glassy eyes stay open wide.
Do they enjoy the view?

*Sweet dreams, fish.*

# Fish

Fish don't have eyelids, so they can't close their eyes when they sleep! Scientists aren't sure if fish truly sleep in the same way as land animals do, but they do know that fish take time to rest. Some fish find a place to hide and nap near logs or coral reefs to stay safe at night. Some rest in shallow water and don't move at all. Still others continue swimming as they rest, but they move very slowly and appear to be in a drowsy state.

The grizzly digs his den with care.
He'll stay all winter long.
Once safe inside he'll curl up snug
until he hears spring's song.

*Sweet dreams, grizzly bear.*

# Grizzly Bear

The grizzly bear lives in the American West and gets its name from its frosted, or grizzled, coat. Scientists question whether grizzlies truly hibernate, but they do agree that the bears fall into a deep winter sleep when food is scarce. While sleeping in winter, a grizzly's heart rate and body functions slow down, and it will not eat, drink, or create waste for several months. Grizzly bears wake up when warmer weather arrives.

The tall giraffe eats leafy greens.

She chews and chews and chews.

Her nights and days are one long graze.

There's little time to snooze.

*Sweet dreams, giraffe.*

# Giraffe

The world's tallest mammal, the giraffe, is a very light sleeper. It can spend sixteen to twenty hours a day browsing for food, leaving little time for rest. The giraffe feeds on acacia and wild apricot trees and also spends a lot of time chewing its cud. When the giraffe does lie down at night, it bends its long neck back over a hind leg, forming an arch. It may nod off into slumber but takes short naps of only a few minutes each. Giraffes live in dry savanna and forest areas of Africa.

A horse can stand when she is tired.
She's built a special way.
She locks her legs to stay in place,
then takes her naps each day.

**Sweet dreams, horse.**

# Horse

Horses are very comfortable sleeping on their feet. Their bones, muscles, and ligaments allow them to relax, yet also remain upright with no danger of falling down. Their bodies are built so they can lock their joints in place. Horses take short naps that add up to just a few hours each day. They may also sleep lying down and can fall into a deeper sleep when they do. But horses in open country like to sleep standing up because they can react to danger more quickly from an upright position.

At night, he sings and hunts for prey.
By day, some hunt for him!
He roosts in trees to hide away
and blends into a limb.

*Sweet dreams, owl.*

## Owl

During the night, owls hunt for food and make deep hoots, chirps, and whistles. After a night of hunting and singing, they move to a daytime roost where they can rest. Many owls choose to roost in trees because their body color and patterns easily blend with tree bark and branches. This natural camouflage helps keep owls safe during the day. Still, owls sleep lightly when the sun is up. They stay alert, opening their eyes now and then to keep watch.

A dolphin swims in blue-green seas.
At times, she's half asleep.
Her brain will rest, yet stay alert
to guide her in the deep.

*Sweet dreams, dolphin.*

## Dolphin

Dolphins spend a lot of time on the move. They dive, swim, surface to breathe, hunt for food, play with other dolphins, and sleep. At rest, they behave very differently from humans. Dolphins sleep with one half of their brain resting and the other half awake. The alert side of the brain keeps watch for predators. It also helps the dolphin swim safely and signals when it is time to surface for air. Various types of dolphins live in fresh or salt water all over the world.

He doesn't need a comfy bed.
So how does this bird doze?
He tucks his bill in soft pink plumes
and strikes a one-legged pose.

*Sweet dreams, flamingo.*

# Flamingo

When the brightly colored flamingo sleeps, it lays its head on its body and tucks one leg under its belly. Scientists believe it stands and rests on one leg to help it stay warmer because it spends so much time in the water. Flamingos alternate the support leg when sleeping so that neither leg becomes too cold. The flamingo is a wading bird and lives in very large flocks near water and mudflats in the tropics.

At times he leaves his lofty perch
to sweep the sky in flight,
but mostly he hangs upside down
and slumbers day and night.

*Sweet dreams, brown bat.*

## Brown Bat

Some bats roost alone, and others gather in groups. They search for
places like caves, hollow trees, or old buildings. These places shelter
them from the sun, rain, cold temperatures, and other animals. Many
bats hang upside down while resting. From this position, it is very easy
for a bat to take off into flight. It will just let go, drop downward, and
begin flapping its wings to take off. Bats are found in most habitats
around the world.

He doesn't have a handmade quilt.
He's covered, without fail.
This fellow curls into a ball—
his blanket is his tail.

*Sweet dreams, anteater.*

# Giant Anteater

Also called antbears, giant anteaters live in Central and South America. When awake and hungry, the anteater uses its long, sticky tongue to scoop up and eat thousands of insects each day. When it is time to sleep, the anteater prefers a quiet location out of sight. Once it finds a spot behind a bush, the giant anteater settles in and sleeps curled up, using its long, bushy tail to cover its head and body.

This seabird soars high in the sky.
She glides with grace and flair.
Her days are spent above the waves.
She naps while in the air!

**Sweet dreams, frigatebird.**

# Magnificent Frigatebird

Magnificent frigatebirds, one of five species of frigatebirds, can be found along tropical coastlines in North and South America. With sturdy wings that span seven feet from tip to tip, the magnificent frigatebird is built for gliding. An expert at riding thermals, this seabird can climb up to one and a half miles above the ocean before it descends. It is unable to land on the water because its feathers are not waterproof. Frigatebirds are on the wing continuously day and night, and scientists believe the birds nap while soaring high in the sky.

The little pups are fast asleep.
Where are they? Look around.
They do not rest in hollow trees.
Their bunk is underground!

**Sweet dreams, prairie dogs.**

# Black-Tailed Prairie Dog

Black-tailed prairie dogs are not actually dogs but large, short-tailed ground squirrels. They are social animals and live in "towns" that may number just a few to thousands of prairie dogs. For shelter and protection, they create long, deep burrows underground with tunnels and nest chambers. They are active during the day and sleep at night. Black-tailed prairie dogs live in the Great Plains of North America and parts of Canada and Mexico.

The walrus snoozes anywhere.
He doesn't fuss or pout.
He hooks his tusks into the ice
and slumbers hanging out!

**Sweet dreams, walrus.**

# Walrus

The walrus is certainly an odd sleeper. It may sleep on land in large groups. It can also sleep underwater, rising for air and sinking back down. Sometimes a walrus even sleeps while floating on its back or belly or by hooking its tusks into ice to stay anchored in place! Living in seawater in the Arctic, the walrus is a very good swimmer but rather clumsy on land. Its sharp tusks do come in handy—they cut through ice, help the walrus defend itself, and are used to pull its huge body out of the water onto ice.

A flock of mallards nestles in.
They doze off one by one.
The ducks along the small group's edge
keep watch 'til morning sun.

*Sweet dreams, mallards.*

# Mallards

Mallard ducks can be found at most ponds or lakes. They usually sleep in a flock at night for protection. The ducks along the outer edge of the flock sleep lightly and open their eyes to look around. The ducks in the middle of the group sleep more deeply. If there is a threat, one or more ducks will sound an alarm. Scientists believe the mallard shuts down one side of its brain for sleep while the other side remains alert.

The animals are sleeping now.
They're resting, just like you.
And as they slumber their own way,
they wish you sweet dreams, too!